**As the Wa**

*10th Anniversary Edition*

annie
here is a Book I have
thought you would have
fun reading. I work
at a Waffle house
and the Book is
right on. We deal
with things like
this every day

Love
Grandma
Syl.

By: Jay M Horne

ISBN: 978-0-9963227-1-3
Library of Congress Control Number: 2018909675

*This work is dedicated to*

those who were there *that* night

*and is written for*

Nancy (Waitress at 3$^{rd}$ Shift Waffle House in Douglasville, GA 2002)

# Preface

Who would have thought a book about Waffle House would have enjoyed so much success? There is something about hanging out under the random flicker of the big yellow sign that never loses its allure to late night drinkers and early morning recovering alcoholics. Hell, you may even come in one midnight as the former, and leave the next morning as the latter, and not just as a customer!

I started writing this special edition after the breaking news story of the man who entered the Waffle House one night and helped himself to the flattop grill and waffle irons while the solitary employee was asleep at the low-top bar. He photo-documented the whole experience on Facebook with his cell phone and left enough money to cover what he cooked and ate. Later he received a call from the district manager and was offered a job critiquing that region's Waffle House locations. It reminded me that Waffle House will never change (and it shouldn't).

My fallback alternative to complete failure was always to go back living in an extended stay motel and work 3rd shift at Waffle House. A plan that unfortunately fell by the wayside when I published the first edition of 'As The Waffle Burns' back in 2009. Apparently, writing a book about the company you work for is considered sabotage? Who would have thought. It was a real bummer to me. I wrote the book during my second bout of employment with the franchise, and what was shocking was that the local management was in on the endeavor and excited about it.

I really loved working the late night, and listening to the unique stories that crossed the high-top. Besides that, flipping spatulas and knives, balancing spoons on my forehead, and juggling shakers made me feel like Tom Cruise in the 1988 movie 'Cocktail'. It wasn't quite Hibachi cooking, but it was fun, and the environment was a bit more forgiving. Plus, no one loves a two bit show like a bunch of lush Hedonists.

When the book was complete, I brought a copy to my manager and let him read it. The plans were to get Waffle House to print table toppers and advertise for the publication. The plans went through, but the table toppers didn't say 'As The Waffle Burns' by Jay Horne, they said 'Big Appetite' by Sam Mcleod.

Supposedly, Joe Rogers, the owner of the Waffle House name, had his own plans while wind was being caught of my writing. Sam Mcleod, a cousin of Joe Rogers, had begun whipping up his own book a little after I started mine. Thing was, I had already purchased all of the key words on Google at the time, and my ad campaign put a damper on their book sales. That is only my theory—but the facts fit. When I came in a few days after giving my manager the book, I was fired and there were a stack of Sam's table toppers in the office. Go figure.

Perhaps with the huge success of my writing, the owners of 'The Awful Waffle' will have had a change of heart. How can you not have a sense of humor when you are attached to the most iconic southern restaurant chain in U.S. History? Since the book's first publication in 2010 the restaurant has sadly been spotlighted for strange acts of gun violence, which can not necessarily be attributed to its operations. Schools, churches, and other well-known organizations have been subject to the same tragedies, yet Waffle House's uniquely cynical vignette brings it national attention. Defamation of the establishment is in no way the intention of this manuscript, quite the contrary is true. With the colored past of documented mishaps and laughable episodes that Waffle House has provided us, a book like this is part of its story—no pun intended.

While the owners of such a franchise may never have this genuine line-cook and lover of the establishment return to their ranks, I will continue to tell the stories that maintain the lifelong tradition of late night interaction between customer and cook. Additional excerpts, headlines, and customer-submitted-photographs with accompanying commentary have been added to the appendix in this new anniversary edition.

If you are in need of enlightenment, a good meal, or simply a laugh, pour yourself into a booth at your nearest Waffle House, crack open these texts to a random story, and relax under the big yellow sign 'As The Waffle Burns'.

# Foreword

Sarcasm has the high seat when it comes to life's highlights. I use to say God took a back seat to sarcasm ages ago but how can that even be said without a little bit of sarcastic twang dripping from the end of the sentence?

Way down here, under the big yellow sign, we have seen all types of comings and goings. Everyone moving, quickly back and forth from there where to's and their gotta get done's. Being in the middle of such riddle I suppose is what sets *us* apart. 'Location, location, location' the saying goes, and where better to be but right smack in the middle of where ever it is you've been and where it is you're going.

*Irony* is a word used in the English language to describe something that explains its opposite, but at Waffle House there's no room for irony here! Only good old fashioned, pure, straight down to the bone sarcasm is accepted here, and don't y'all forget it!

# Table Of Contents

# Introduction

Life's a joke, so let us start here:

What has six arms, six legs, six tits, and six teeth?

Answer: 3rd Shift at the Waffle House

Go ahead laugh it out, and if you're the waitress (or cook) with the 'oh so snaggly teeth', keep smiling, I'm on your side, I promise.  You're gonna have your annoyingly stereotypical Waffle House crew waiting on you or working with you one time or another, that's guaranteed!  On the other side of the counter, the customer side, there will always be the 'Thrice a dayer'.  The old man who is there in the morning for breakfast, then back for lunch, and again for dinner.  Yep.  Then you have the folks with bartender syndrome who always ask why.

The question sticks in our human consciousness like dry grits, and always represents itself with perfect enough timing to get under our skin, over and over again.

## WHY?

Why did he have to die?

Why did I marry this guy?

Why do I try so hard and get nowhere?

Why are we here?

Why do I have it so bad?

Why do I work all day?

Why can't I just be happy?

Why am I always hungry?

Why?

Why?

Why?

And this is no less than a perfect introduction for the second in the line-up of our tragic tales in our Waffle House saga starting on page 15:

Why ask why?

But let us first consider, what about our comfy Waffle House restaurant environment, gives rise to these tales.

# Tragic Tales

Environment is typically the leading factor in our inspiration. Perhaps being particularly close to a Wal-Mart has some influence on the types of tales that come our way, but not *every* Waffle House is born in a Wal-Mart parking lot. Some of our restaurants are located in the remotest locations and still breed the same cesspool of individuality and peculiar family ties. Take Corsica, Texas for example. It is probably one the loneliest of our locations, its only neighbor for miles being the Comfort Inn, but you could bet your wide ass that it will see its share of tragic tales, just as well as any other Waffle House. Perhaps it is all due to the fact that we all sit beneath that big yellow sign. Yellow being a color of cowardice maybe has doomed our regulars into not having the gal to stand up for themselves and in turn allowing themselves to be utterly spent by their own lives. Who knows.

Everything happens for a reason, right? Does being the good guy really pay off in the end? We all like to think so and for our sakes and the sakes of those who have crossed our welcome mat, let us hope.

So you've worked for the awful waffle for the better part of ten years, huh? We would say *that* is tragic enough. Hahaha. Though let us imagine, for a moment, being on the other side of the counter. Here we are having been a Waffle House customer everyday for the better part of ten years. What happened in our existence that finally drove us this deeply in to insanity where we would call this a life, much less, a wonderful life?

The stories collected herein, as I experienced my second bout of employment at the Waffle House may not necessarily be edge of your seat material. But the stories you will read are real. They are all human, emotional, and yes- from the seats of classic Waffle House frequenters. The reviews I have gotten have been mixed, but everyone seems to enjoy the back matter which is chock full of laughs relating to the good old Awful Waffle. I still hold to the belief that Waffle House would have been better off endorsing 'As the Waffle Burns' rather than the owner's nephew's book 'A Southern Fried Life'. This book was released prior to his and written with the knowledge of Waffle House management during its production. So enjoy. Let us know how we are doing and please visit or website www.asthewaffleburns.com to have your pictures and stories show up in our next publication.

With that, begins our tales of tragedy, straight from the customer's mouths, recorded for your pleasure by your friendly local Waffle House cook, right here under the big yellow sign.

# Why ask why?

## By: Diane

People always said good things occur in three's. "Well, I had three husbands and loved each one for a different reason other than love." She says. She goes on to tell me that her first husband was Lust, and still is, "Damn he fine! That was it" She says. Her second was fear. Fear that if she didn't stick to her exact schedule and answer the phone at the right time, every time, it was her ass that was beaten down. "And you vow to care for him and to *serve* him' who put that shit in the wedding vows?! Hell nah, I done had my ass beat, wasn't no love there." She carries on as her hips move slowly, but ever so gently matching the motion of her lips as she speaks.

This lady, has been through the ringer, no doubt! But her body is a dance. She is *slow*, and for sure. "And the third man… I married him for his money." A smug grin at the last comment left her audience wondering if she had always been this truthful. "You damn straight I've been truthful. I done learned!" She dusts off her shoulders, "I even told that man *why* I was marrying him. Fo tha money." That smug grin again, this time matter-of-factly. "My dress was getting hemmed up and my momma gonna say to me 'You just marrying that man for his money' as she zipped it up in back."

A voice breaks from across the room, "And a mother should never tell her child that!"

"Right" says Shanique. People are now getting settled in to the subject. We know truth when we hear it. Interesting truth is even better.

We are all here sitting at the Waffle House having a human conversation with, what may be, the biggest question mark in human history.

"Clayton was his name." The voice from across the room would eventually begin her story, but not quiet yet.

"I had done been through enough hard times to know what I wuz doing. This time I was right and I knew it! I would prove my momma wrong! I would *NOT* marry this man for his money even if that had been my plan!" Shanique pauses, rolls her eyes up and tucks her chin down before she tells us, "Oh we married! But I would doom my life by living those years like money didn't matter." She glances over at the old lady that had interrupted her, motioning for her to continue for her.

17

"All because you wanted to prove your Mom wrong. It doesn't matter what you tell your children they will do the exact opposite to prove it was *their* own decision."

This time it is Shanique who interrupts the old woman, who obviously knew from experience what she was talking about, "Exactly! Even though I had told the man myself that was why I was marryin' him. But maybe, just maybe, I wouldn't have gone through with the whole thing if momma woulda just kept her mouth shut!" Everyone is amused. The room is filled with smiles and nods.

You can always trust Waffle House to bring you some interesting stories and experiences. Being right next to a Wal-Mart presents us a frequent supply of rare characters as well. If you want to know how strange then check out that old web site;

www.peopleofwalmart.com.

Strange and rare are in no way *bad*. People are people, they are born in different places and at different times, so no two are just alike. They do say variety is the spice of life, right.

On this particular day and during this particular conversation I would realize that the question *why* can hold you down or pick you up depending on how you ask it. The old lady that had joined Shanique in her little spat about Love was carrying with her the weight of the world, and no one even knew it as she greeted customers on a daily basis at the next door Wal-Mart which I so briefly mentioned before. This little miss, was a bit over weight but soft spoken and respectful. She *knew* something.

"I can agree with you because I know a thing or two about being a mother myself." The little old lady had been busy eating the food I had prepared for her. She continued, "I saw a sign for missing children just the other day as I walked in work that had my son's exact first and last name on it. It made me do a double take."

As she pats her lips with her napkin I ask, "Did it look anything like him?"

Shaking her head, "Lord no. It just made me feel thankful that I knew where my son was, and send some prayers the way of that poor child's mother."

I have always envied commendable people who are thankful and think first about others. Not that I don't try and act the same way, but I can't seem to drop the belief that others have an easier time at it.

Mary was this little old ladies name, which I would find out a bit later. "From the first day my boy laid foot on this planet I never spoke a bit of baby talk to him." Mary kept on for awhile, "He was like a little man. I could tell from the day I met him. When my next door neighbors had their twins I brought little Clayton with me to meet them first hand."

I couldn't help but ask her if it was the same Clayton that managed our store there. "Let me assure you, that would be impossible." She tells me and then, "The twins we met were both little girls. Pink as could be, and the sweetest little things. Of course, their parents were baby talking to them with their 'goo gagas' and such. I couldn't help but do the same." The expression she made while she demonstrated the act was noticeably typical of any mother. Mary was surely a great story teller and we, engulfed as we are, let her continue. "Clayton was watching me the whole time with curiosity but it wasn't until the ride home he would ask me 'Mom why didn't you baby talk me like you did those babies?' So I explained in words he could understand easily." She prepared herself for the punch line, "Well Clayton baby, you just never struck me as the kind of baby that I should baby talk to." Then that unmistakable Goo goo gaga face assumed her expression, "But I'll talk baby talk to you if you wan me ta talk baby talk to you pumpkin" She says in her best pidlly little baby voice. "At that point Clayton's face curled into a revolting pungent expression and as he recoiled he said shortly, 'No!'" All of us begin laughing at this point and Waffle house is filled with a conglomeration of understanding.

I gathered Clayton was surely a special kid by what she had proclaimed. The intelligence he showed at that young age was due to his odds of birth. Mary was 33 when she became pregnant and after a sonogram and a routine inspection the doctor explained that he would be born with either autism or a high I.Q. The only option at the time was a live abortion where they induce labor and crush the head after it emerges. This was horrible to her ears, so when she heard the offer of adoption, it was considerably juggled about in her mind. The father was a dead beat. But in the end she would decide that she would keep this child and find out what reason God had for him in her life.

"You had a deadbeat in your life too, eh?" Shanique asks while she has a chance.

Mary pats her lips again and with a quick shake of her head she resumes, "Yeah, but lord knows I didn't marry him. Couldn't. He never gave me the time of day after our one night together. I was already old honey, but after deciding to keep little old Clayton in my life I felt more blessed than depressed." Mary looks down below her table as if expecting to find something there, "I have some photos in my purse, but it's in the car. The strangest thing about Clayton is that people could not resist his draw. We would be in a parking lot loading groceries and strangers would always come by just to pat his head, like they felt how special he was."

The same few customers were still engulfed in this ladies story and no one had entered since I served the last guest, so I dared a bit closer to get it on the action. Mary saw me walking over and unexpectedly asked me, "How old are you son?"

I paused close to the register and leaning on one arm answered politely, "Twenty nine." Feeling that she must think I hadn't been paying attention I ventured a question of my own, "How old is Clayton?"

There was no pause in her answer, "Twenty seven last Friday."

Shanique, hearing the talk of Mary's special son knew all too well the feeling of giving birth to the next great. Sliding her seat back, she began to stand, "Well, I had thirteen of my own." Hushed gasps came from those present, nothing Shanique hadn't learned to block out years ago, I'm sure. "The eldest of mine is the same age of my boyfriend." She smiles reminiscing. "That's what I always felt I was meant for, to make babies." At this point Mary silently vacates her seat and heads for the door. Her jacket still draped across her chair was a sure sign she wasn't going far. Shanique is taking advantage of the moment by putting a thing or two in about her own saga, "Now don't go think I do it for the government benefits, cuz I don't. All my babies are with their fathers who make the ends meet, I just like child bearing." A slight pause to let us react, but no one does, "Not to say I haven't had my share of tragic moments. I like to say I have thirteen children, cuz that's the number I gave birth to. But only three is living. Some died at childbirth, one was beat to death by their step father. Others, well, tragedy is something worth speaking of I reckon, but a whole lot harder to do when it comes in multiples." The group of patrons and employees now standing in ear shot couldn't help but assume that classic face, the face of confusion, disappointment, and sorrow. It is really a mix of the three because no one knows how to respond to a person of such strength. Do you console them when it looks as if they have overcome this calamity? Maybe their stern face is just a front, maybe inside they still feel the reckless abandon of their God or faith. Either way, we all sat silent, only to be saved by the sound of the door opening and Mary reassuming her place among us.

"I am sorry I had to excuse myself for a moment." Mary settled herself into her chair again as I noticed photos in her hand.

"Oh, you brought us some photos to look at?" I asked, to break the uneasy feeling in the room. She hands me one as people come closer to look at the kid she called angelic in his charisma.

"That's him."

The people passed about the photos she had brought in, but I couldn't seem to let this one I started with go. All of the pictures were when he was between three and five years old. He truly did have a glow about him. After everything I had heard and pictured in my mind, he was definitely a god send to this lady. I looked up at her after a long time with this picture and just had to ask the pressing question on everyone's mind, "So where is he now? What is he doing?"

Again, no pause before her response, "He's dead. Hung himself on a swing set at seven years old."

The room assumed again that mix of emotions. But the faces— the faces told more this time. We all could sense the huge weight this lady had carried with her all these years. This time the response was in grained in each human there. We all hugged her.

It was only natural for the people who had gathered to start clearing out quickly, but I sat with her a few more moments. In the end I remembered what she left me with. She had said to me, "I brought that boy into this world because I knew God had something special planned for his life. I am still waiting to find out what it is."

This is when it struck me, the awful truth. Mary has been carrying on for twenty some odd years trying to answer this question - "WHY?"

The human psyche is so complex and massively inconceivable that there are over jillians of different outcomes for any one situation at any one time. We narrow down our choices in nano seconds and pick through them quickly with our feelings, sometimes accompanied by thought, and end up with a result. But, still those choices were there for a time. They were technically 'thunk' up, but just never acted upon and in turn never experienced.

We are all parts of the project. I am not talking about 'the projects' where countless hours of hands hard at work go unnoticed and unclocked by the bosses watch, but *THE project*, **YOUR** *Project*. That project *is* whatever it is you happen to find yourself doing at the time. It's your life to live. Live it!

The *present* was and always has been your birthday present, from GOD.

If that don't sink in then I think we could all use a little bit of advice from our old buddy Budweiser:

'Why ask why, try bud dry'

# THE WAFFLE HOUSE RESEARCH PROJECT

By: Jay

I'm a *nice guy*.

Everyone seems to get a kick out of my unfortunate predicaments. It seems I am always making someone crack a smile when I tell them my stories. I just have that effect on people. Then again, I also seem to piss everyone off that I meet as well.

I one time, considered wearing a shirt with the disclaimer:

It may not be my fault, it may not be right now, but eventually, I'll piss ya off.

I'm not sure exactly why it is this happens. I reckon it has something to do with people not being happy unless everyone around them has a life just as miserable as their own. I bet you know exactly what I'm talking about here. Ya ever watched someone get angry with you because you were happy *all* the time? Yep. It's like the same thought runs through everyone's' head once in a while. It goes something like:

"I am happy your happy, but if you were in my shoes you would be the most unappreciated son-of-a-bitch on the planet. "

From this point of view you can see how being a nice guy may end up landing you in last place, or at minimum, the target of every miserable soul around you. But there is one thing that is great about being 'last'. And that's having the last *Laugh*!

"Do you think you *know* somebody? You're wrong. Nineteen years I laughed and smiled with my significant other and then in a matter of two hours, I found myself used, accused, and abused."

-Glen Scott

Obviously, he wasn't amused.

## *Another customer story:*

Glen was a rancher by trade. He owned a stump grinding business, drove an F-350, and his conversations always included the goings on of the local feed store or the handling of his horses. To this day when I see the dip in a horse's spine I think of Glen. God knows how he didn't break the back of any horse he sat atop.

As he stared dead ahead, over his cup of coffee he recounted the events that led him to the Waffle House for the first time, not long ago.

"Your life is the epitome of happiness. You have what some would call the perfect home. A house, money, a wife and 19 years of loyalty and respect." he started

"I am 65 years old, and if you would have woke me up in the middle of the night and said my wife would be leaving me that morning I would have called you a damn LIE!

"It wasn't two weeks ago that my son-in-law called asking for financial help. The good lord in heaven sees to it that everyone has a stumbling block or two to help em grow along the way, but this kid had had many. I try my best not to judge a book by its cover and to never be stereotypical and such things. But this boy just wasn't right from the get go. A couple of run-ins with the law, and a drug charge on him later left me weary and losing patience with him to say the least. Most of all, my wife was getting stressed out about the whole deal. She loved her son, as a mother loves any of her youngins. But sometimes even a mother's will can't sway the will of God."

The white ribbon of steam has thinned and twists out from between his hands as he grips his mug.

"My wife and I never shared a crossed word with one another. We were as two peas in a pod, a fork and a spoon, or what have you. But that day I told that boy he'd better shape up or ship out his momma was in between me and him in a flash. Call him the butter knife to complete the set. Now mamma weighs a good 195 and I myself am a good 250. We're hefty folks, grant it. But I'll swear to you beyond the grave I didn't shove that lady. She getting amongst us, caught her slipper on the lip of the trailer door, and before anything could be said she was a lying on the ground in agony.

"Of course, my first reaction was to tend to my wife, but her son-in-law was younger, and much spryer. 'You bastard! You pushed my mom!' He'd yelp. 'Oh, Momma, are you okay, we'll get him for this.' He was a regular old Tom Cruise, or Hanks, have your pick."

Glen actually looked up to my eyes with that. I stood silent, rolling the dishcloth in my hands until he continued.

"I was flabbergasted. Not so much at what he was saying, but what she did, 'Call the law!' She'd said. I stood there in that doorway; mind you, I filled every inch of that port as the breath in my lungs dropped heavily. I could not believe what I was seeing and hearing. My wife, my sweet lovely wife, of almost twenty years is blurting out call the law, as her piece of shit ex-con son sits over her laying the blame in my direction?! How did this happen?

"In no time, I was behind bars for a crime I didn't commit, and while I tried my damnedest to get out, *she* would be liquidating our checking account and clearing out my house of everything I owned. She even took my damn dog! By the time I got out of the local lock up and realized what had happened, I could do nothing more than come here to the Waffle House and sit over my cup of Joe. You think you know someone."

Glen recounted that one night as I worked the nine to seven shift when I first started this job. How this man had his last laugh is a whole different story, but it sparked in me the drive in generating my own melodramatic experience while I worked under the Yellow Sign.

What I call my 'Waffle House Research Project Experience' is recorded in full account below. The goal was to be the nicest guy I could possibly be, like Glen, and see where it led me. Anyone with half a brain knows, in an environment like the Waffle, niceness will be considered weakness and you will be used and abused. What the heck, I have time on my hands, and it will make for a good book!

## *My story:*

My name is Jay. I will tell you now I am not the most gentle looking person in the world. My life has been long, and the road rough. A few years back I found my niche in the writing and publishing industry and started making easier money. I say *easy* money, but what I mean is, a more bearable way to make enough income to support me and my loved ones, as long as I don't stop working.

I had been alone all my life, right up into my twenties, that's when I met her. I knew from the second I laid eyes on her that she was what would turn me right. I had, until that time treated myself like hell, literally. Years and years would pass before one little phrase would finally become bold enough, in my mind, to make me change. The phrase was this:

"Treat people like you want to be treated"

I know what you're thinking. Everyone has heard this phrase at one point in their lifetime or another, but it wouldn't sink in until the image in the mirror looking back at me was crying out for help. I looked at my pathetic reflection and realized that the catch phrase applies also to yourself.

I am also an *attractive* guy.

I always was an attractive guy, I heard it all the time. My mother when I was young, in to my twenties. My friends and co-workers, while I worked my petty hourly wage jobs and lived in cheap apartments and hotels. So I never thought my looks had anything to do with the fact I never shared my life with another. I suppose, my first few relationships affected my mentality in some way shape or form.

The first girl I kissed, was a perfect start to my tragic love life. She kissed me subtly at ten years old and left at the end of the community dance. We had professed our love to one another that night, after weeks of stolen glances across the cafeteria at school. The following Monday would bring my first relationship when we got back to school. What a perfect one it would be!

When Monday arrived, it came with my first heartache. She would never show up. I learned from a friend a few days later that she had been sent off to another state to live with her father. Now, as wretched as that is to a little man, I didn't entirely lose hope. I would try and love again but it would be years later. Seven years to be exact. At that point, hormones raging, my first taste of sexuality came with an overload of selfishness. I would leave home at seventeen to be with a girl who claimed her love for me. Selfish as I was, I would up and leave my family with not so much as a word, thinking I had found the love of my life.

As a young man, I wouldn't quite understand that Love is something that you should spread out amongst those close to you. My love went from my family to that girl. I shut off my family and focused my entire being on the new found me and mine. In the end, despite my family's effort to reconnect with me, the second 'so called' love of my life would lead me on for nine months before cheating on me and sending me home with my tail between my legs. Moving out of state was the only option to keep my friends and family free of abusive and threatening phone calls from her friends.

It would be months later that I would meet my fiancée. She was no less than everything a man could want. Smart, funny, pretty, nurturing, loyal, she had it all. The only problem was, our first night together started with her telling me, "Promise me this won't be a one time thing." So *I* take the blame for this one going bad. I never should have nodded. Five years later, I would be in the Navy while I kicked drug addiction and alcoholism. She would finally wise up and leave me, just as I figured out that she was the best thing that ever happened to me. That was my regret that I knew would return to me as bad karma—and it did!

Kicking myself in the ass for my loss was easy over the next few years. The act consisted of over the counter drugs, prescription medication, and booze. Of course, that would lead me to all the wrong people, including my next attempted relationship with a convenient store clerk who already had three kids, and would miscarry mine by smoking the pipe and snorting the powder. Good thing, because when I caught her abusing drugs in the back of a friends car with her daughter sitting in her lap, and mine in her belly, I ripped my keys from her hands and told her to get lost forever.

Years would pass. I finally, tried my hand at another relationship when I was twenty-five years old. That brings us back to *her*. I got on with this Australian girl, who was smart and fun. I really poured myself into that relationship, thinking finally, that I was *ready*. Ready for marriage, ready for children, ready for the whole nine yards. Two years later, I find out, she wasn't!

So, My life had been a one-way train to tragic endings. I think the reason I turned so much inward was because I really needed to find myself amongst the wreckage. Writing was my way of doing that. Then, when presented with *this* unique opportunity to test the human spirit, I couldn't help but jump on board..

Now that you have a bit of background on me, let us now get down to the matter at hand. Allow me to introduce my Waffle house crew.

First and foremost, I must introduce our manager. Barron is a loveable guy. He hired me on the spot. I guess when you have books published around the world, it is a bit enticing to a young manager to perhaps end up in one. Congrats, my friend you made it! For real though, he was probably not impressed in the least about my past achievements, we just had a heart to heart, and honesty won him over. That is what I like to tell myself anyhow. Barron is twenty three years old. Surprise, surprise right. Now-a-days if you work for someone older than you, you better be getting paid more than minimum wage! Else, how will you get compensated for all the technical training you will have to volunteer just to make your job easier?!

Standing at the flat top on first shift brought back a flood of memories. I had worked for an Awful Waffle ten years previous, when I had my first inspirational break in writing. As we stood elbow to elbow cooking for the masses, Barron would lean over with tidbits of advice ever so often. This I am sure was a luxury to him, considering most people he had been training lately had probably been standing there trying to crack an egg for their full first shift! No offense guys, I been there, done that. I knew I would like working with the guy because he was easy going, and kept me laughing. I remember, in the middle of the rush as I heated the pan for an omelet he tells me that it's ready.

"How do you know?" I ask.

At this point, I hadn't dropped a bit of egg in the oil to see if it was hot enough to put the whisked omelet in yet. Dropping some egg white in your oil is a sure way to tell if the oil is at the right temperature to put in your omelet mix. If it simmers, it's ready to roll.

Barron grabs the pan and swirls it a bit with his right hand. The oil slides around the edges like filtered water.

"You see on the edge, how the oil ribbons up as you turn it?" He asks.

"Yeah. Yeah." I say, after making sure I wasn't lying my ass off just to move the conversation forward. A habit of mine.

Remember: *I am on a mission to be the perfectly friendly person. That means utterly honest as well.*

"So, you can tell if the oils ready by just looking at?" I ask.

"It's an art Jay. You work with it for a while and eventually you know what it's telling you."

Barron goes on to explain his experience of cooking on a cruise ship and high scale restaurants. Impressive to say the least. Not so much as the kind of training that he has been exposed to, as to the training he has retained! Oh what I would give for a young mind again!

"So." I say, "I should be able to tell when the oil is ready."

Barron looks at me like I can only imagine the horse whisperer looks at his horse, "You have to listen to the oil. It will tell you when it's ready." We laugh. Two days later on a shift by myself I find myself mumbling,

"I need a damn miracle ear!"

Barron is a good hearted, deserving individual. He lets the ladies walk all over him, to a point, but that's a sure sign of good leadership skills, or at least, strong mental fortitude!

The first person who really left a lasting impression on me following Barron was this guy named Davin. What made him stand out to me was the advice he gave me while I worked first shift with him.

"These girls will give you hell if you let him," he would say, "but just take it with a grain of salt and fire right back at 'em with a sarcastic comment." He raised his eyebrows with a glance over in Trixies direction, "Take Trixie for example. She always has something negative to say or complain about. Maybe if she lost some of that extra 200 pounds of weight she's carrying around she would be a bit less miserable."

His cackle was a laugh to be envious of and I couldn't help but join in.

He continues, "I think with that red hair, muffin top body, and melodramatic attitude she would better fit in a B-Movie than third shift at Waffle House." Again that laugh.

Davin was not a *bad* looking guy, just a bit over weight and a tad bit scruffy. His dream was making it to the big time with his band, which I had the pleasure of listening to, during my time here at Waffle House. I didn't, however, have the heart to tell him they weren't going anywhere with him being the solo singer. Again, my research project rules were to be nice, and so I told them they were fantastic. Kinda a conflict with rule number two, *be utterly honest*, but I wasn't telling them anything they weren't already delusional of to begin with.

Davin looks over to me as he flips the bacon on the flat top, "The real trick in dealing with Trixie is to upset her more than she already is when she starts giving you hell. I usual comeback with something like 'Shouldn't you be out back snorting around for some truffles?' or

'Shouldn't you be out back sharpening your tusk on a root?"' My laugh drowned his out this time. Waffle House—characters welcome.

I knew Davin was on his way out the door when I began observing him straying from his own advice. He never took things with a grain of salt, and I rarely heard him directly retaliate against those banshees of waitresses. I, on the other hand, heeded his advice and it seemed to be working fairly well. Sometimes, I could sense the tension in him as he cooked by me. He would walk to the back fuming, or be mumbling under his breath. The only outlet he had was complaining to me, which I gladly let him do with a smile and, at times, a laugh. In the end he would try transferring stores to extend his inevitable departure from the Awful, but eventually, eventually, it's gonna piss ya off.

Needless to say, after being fired for a no call no show, his girlfriend, who was also employed with yours truly, would stand up for him and get herself canned as well. Cops actually escorted her off the property.

Julie and Davin were a match mate in heaven. Davin constantly complaining about how he didn't want to be around Julie, and Julie complaining about Davin not wanting to be around her. Who could've blamed him, she could literally drive you up a wall with conversation. You know the kind of person I am talking about. Someone who has to stand within three inches from you to talk to you and lean in nose to nose in order to make sure your listening. Her bottom teeth were nearly eroded away entirely, which at least gave you the sense that maybe you should be holding your breath. Do I say these things to people? Of course not. But now that I am done with my research project, there are no holds barred.

In fact, during my little project, I went all out and did something completely selfless to ensure this girl's happiness. Her children had been badly burned in a fire, from where someone in her household left a butane can too close to the camp fire. Upon, hearing about it, a fellow co-worker and myself decided to drive the four hundred miles to visit her and her children in the hospital. At the time, Davin was on the rocks with her, and she was left all alone with her burned children. No one was going to visit her, so Carol and I opened our hearts to the situation on our days off.

Carol is a character, to say the least. If driving an hour and a half to work and back at the Waffle House isn't enough to give you color then toss in four and a half feet of shining light and twice as much self pity. If anyone could relate with me while I did my time at the Awful Waffle, it would have to be her. She gave her all to the world around her everyday and constantly acted as a shield for co-workers by stepping in front of verbal bullets without question. How did she do it? Well, first of all, despite her own misfortune, she would laugh. Not the laugh you'd expect from a four and a half foot skinny blonde, but the laugh you'd expect from a teenage girl on mushrooms. She laughed about laughing! All the laughing she did, grew her heart so big, she was actually willing to sacrifice her time off to go out of her way and visit a person in need. What better way to do some research?!

We left around noon. Carol had been a great friend, to say the least. Hard working and a joy to be around. Her selfless act of driving all the way out to see this girl and her children was nothing less than amazing. Besides, I had a few people I needed to visit around the Atlanta area in regards to a book of mine, so, we figured make a trip out of it. She showed up at my folks' house to pick me up, and after calling Davin to see if he wanted to send flowers or anything with us, we were gone in a flash. Of course he didn't. This was more or less a path for him to get out of this relationship and on with his own life. The drive took us about six hours, and when the hospital finally came in view we were in much need of a stretch.

Julie sat alone in the waiting room when we walked in. Obviously, she had been alone and without sleep for days, unable to see her injured children. We hugged her and sat with her as she chatted on her phone with numerous relatives.

It was hard for Carol and I to witness someone in such despair. We both have had our shares of ruin, and seeing someone so down on their luck was only an open doorway for us to maybe heal a bit of the world that had so treated us the same many times before. I decided I would get us a hotel room so that Julie could sleep in a real bed. Carol and I were going to share a bed, as per her request. But, in the end, Carol has me lay with Julie because she is feeling sorry for her. Just comfort mind you, but we all could have used a bit of human contact that night. Laying with Julie wasn't the most comfortable thing I had ever done. But I did it. She kissed me, and I let her. I thought rejection would be just another brick on the stack at this point. I fell asleep quickly so things wouldn't elevate.

The next morning Carol and I were headed off to East Atlanta for my business deal. Julie told us that her uncle was showing up shortly so we left ten minutes before his supposed arrival. We all exchanged hugs, I kissed her and we said "Goodbye".

Driving through Atlanta was uneventful for us. We had both seen the 8 lane highways moving at 100 miles per hour before. It wouldn't be long until we were smack in the middle of Douglas county and back to my old stomping grounds. Carol would leave me here with my friends, who had their band's first premier show the next night, and drive back home in fear she might ruin our good time. Later that night I set a date with my editor, Denika, to go to the club before catching the bus home in a couple of days.

Now, here I lay on the couch at my friend Tony's house after the band's debut had been canceled. Everyone is sleeping and my mind is running wild. The phone rings. It's Julie. I ask her what she's doing and she informs me that her relatives never showed up that night. Her uncle was suppose to show up in a couple of days and take her back to Florida. My mind swirls as I talk with her. I am *utterly* faced with an option. Number one, wait here at my friends house and go on the date with my editor returning home thereafter by bus, or, number two, stick to my project and do 'the right thing' by returning to Gainesville by bus and being with her until her family arrives. Here I am, stuck in a catch twenty-two. I kissed her last night, so that obligates me to be a caring person or throw away every good deed I have thus far accomplished. I throw my arms up in irony, and take it with a grain of salt. I'd be on the bus back to her tomorrow.

The next few days were no less than hell. A ride on a Greyhound bus and two straight days in a hospital room with no change of clothes or shower isn't exactly what you'd call vacation. Her son was getting better every day, and I found a lot of joy in trying to make him feel better. He was a tough kid.

By the time her uncle showed up on Valentine's day I was utterly exhausted. Any time I would begin to nod off I would be awakened by Julie and her, "You don't sleep if I don't!"

I would have given my left nut for a pair of ruby slippers that I could tap three times! It was directly before her son's release when Davin called. He was going on about how he wanted another chance and how she shouldn't break up their family. I could hear his voice coming through the phone as he spoke. Music to my ears, I thought as I laughed inside.

She turns to me and asks solemnly, "Would you be mad if I gave him one more chance?"

I sighed, put on my best face and said, "Of course not! I was hoping you two would work it out. Your family deserves a second chance."

She smiled as she relayed the news to Davin. She walks out of the room to talk.

Her uncle leans close to me and asks, "Did she just break up with you?"

A shit eatin' grin occupies my face as I nod and say, "Something like that."

I can see her uncle's mind hard at work but he won't say what he thinks. I sit back in my chair full of relief and smiling inside, knowing full well that he is sitting across from me thinking, "What a kick in the nuts! Come be with this girl and her kids in place of her shit boyfriend, and she breaks up with you to get back with him on Valentine's day?!"

I feel great. I smile within as I think up the title of my little project - '**Misunderstood**'.


It takes approximately fifteen hours to get home from Gainesville. I am dirty, stinky, hungry, broke, tired (thank God!), and in the company of those who constantly talk about how no *man* should come between those kids and Julie (The man, being me and/or Davin). Stress isn't even the word here. I sleep all I can. Ironically, we stop five times during our fifteen-hour commute at ... YOU GUESSED IT-

# WAFFLE HOUSE!

For the sake of argument I stand out in the cold, watching the baby through the window of the car while the family sits inside the Awful Waffle drinking warm java and having jovial conversation with the waitresses. Okay, so they're not breaking the law because the car is running and I am keeping an eye on the kid while they spend thirty minutes inside a Waffle House, but should you be? My sympathy for the child runs deeper than I ever thought possible. The kid has just survived an explosion, and has spent the last week and a half in the hospital bed. Now, here he sits asleep in his car seat with a guy who's only known him for a week starring at him through the window of a strange car, waiting patiently for the three he knows best to finish their thirty-minute conversation and cup of joe inside the damn Waffle House!

The last thing I want to do is open the car-door and get in beside him, because I am afraid of waking him and returning him to his misery. Instead, I stand outside the car and freeze while keeping a watchful eye on him and a warm thought for him in my heart. Of course, no one even glances my direction or thinks of what the baby or *I* may be doing. They continue on in their comfort, totally immersed in their own future lives.

I would arrive home in time for work but not without grief. Apparently, Davin had been calling the Waffle House to vent with his problems and in-turn rumors had spread about me somehow being the bad person in all of this! The story would be completely turned upside down. Now, all of a sudden it was as if I used Carol for a ride to Georgia to sleep with Julie and ruin her relationship with her boyfriend amidst a tragedy! And this was only one card that was dealt in my direction for the invisible nametag I would eventually bare.

The next card dealt came from Shannon. You might say that Shannon was a cute little thing, but you'd follow it up by stating that she's also a HUGE bitch! Just turning eighteen is her entire arsenal. She loves to boast about the fact that she gets hit on every day at work, which by the way, is a little less than an accomplishment, seeing as most of her suitors have more pimples than they do teeth. She would *finally* settle for some young Asian lad whom she met in Catholic school. That match mate in heaven would be kicked out of that same school for pre-marital relations in the house of God.

Shanique, was introduced *way* earlier on in the story why ask why. You remember the one who tucks her chin down and is slow and fo' Sho'? Well, come to find out she has a bit of a problem with telling fibs. Pathological liar, I believe is how Shannon will eventually put it to me. To each their own, but one in particular fib started up a mess that dealt out card two.

Shanique, being the pathological liar that she is, one day tells me that she overheard Shannon saying, "I like Jay. If I were going to cheat on my boyfriend, it would be with Jay." Now, upon hearing this, I began debating with Shanique Shannon's ordeal. Shannon is currently engaged to this Chinaman and is frequently heard speaking of her doubts on the matter. So, for me to hear something like Shaniques last statement gets me thinking ... If Shannon isn't truly happy with this guy, maybe she is looking for a way out. Being the kind I am, I would hate to see someone go through a marriage they really didn't have their heart in, just for the sake of saving face. So I wrote a letter to Shannon.

The next day upon entering the house de la waffle there was numerous accounts of people who had read the letter, which was no big deal to me. It was honesty based on a lie I didn't know of at the time. A close friend of mine, however, discloses to me that Shannon's account of the letter was a bit off key to the manager. When I heard what she had told him, and found out that she was backed by Trixie's inconceivable plights, I determined it was time for some action.

Trixie is the type of person that belongs in a B-Movie rather than a Waffle House. She's six foot three and as stated before, over weight. Her red hair and Irish complexion add to her comical, yet miserable persona. The fact that she goes to my manager and complains that I was hitting on her when I found out that she broke up with her boyfriend has nothing to do with the way I describe her. Even so, that drew card number three. I think when she heard of the letter I wrote to Shannon she immediately tried to jump in on the drama. And for the record; she described my come on as; 'He looked me up and down like a fresh piece of meat'. I thought to myself, 'My eyes have to do a bit of traveling just to take in her whole girth.' But that's right, I did write a letter to Shannon, I admit that is full truth.

Being a writer for a living, you learn to document everything you put into writ. Letters to individuals are no exception. You never know who might call the national Enquirer or so on and so forth, just for shits and giggles. So I go to my vehicle, bring in my laptop and show my manager the original letter (found on the next page) myself. Problem solved.

Though the management knows I'm sane, there is still quite the whisper going around the restaurant about me. No one knows quite what to make of me. Everything is hearsay, and my actions are always honest in retrospect. So I leave things to simmer, despite knowing that now three cards had been dealt in my direction labeling me as a desperate loner who hits on every susceptible Waffle House girl.

Isn't it funny how sometimes it is the prayers that go unanswered that we are most thankful for?

Dear Shannon,

I know my gift wasn't the best of the best or anything, but believe it or not I was trying to do something extra special for you. I believe everyone has within them a beautiful light and each of us is a whole lot more special than we think. I laughed today when I heard you once again say, "I still think you're going to grow up to be a lonely man with cats." I always laugh. Laugh at something and it can't control you. Besides laughter is God's way of expressing himself, and the best exercise you can get:.

Believe it or not Shannon, I already have grown into that lonely man you speak of. I see myself there everyday. Would I sacrifice my pleasurable tendencies and take someone out that is as unappealing to me as Theresa? No. That would but be diluting an already perfect picture of what I see my future should withhold. You said to me, "I thought you were cute when you first started here." I look at that statement and feel the story of my life unfold in bitterness. Yeah, ya know if I just never did anything or said anything then maybe you would have gone on liking me and thinking I was cute. But LO and behold Jay opens his mouth and acts like his 'Love will never happen to me' self and overlooks someone who is more beautiful than a summer day.

I have prayed for years to find a person who still values love and marriage. A person who can stand up for herself and her chastity. A person who is pleasing to my eyes. A person who can be my friend. A person who can fall in Love. A person to grow with.

All these things must have remained uncertain between us for life to go on in harmony. You haven't seen the whole real me. I have been putting up a huge wall between us. I heard something today that made me think you may have not such a large guard as I foretold. It all left me thinking, 'What if?' and the thing I am left wanting to say more than anything to you is this:

"I see you ending up in an unhappy marriage with a child and a yearning that you deserved better."

"I'll have my cats. You'll have your hubby and children."

all because you think you HAVE to make marriage work and I think no one will ever take it seriously with me.

My parents have been happily married 50 years. That is all I know.

I want a dog. I want a girlfriend. I want a family. A home. A life. A wife.

You don't even know me. I don't even know you. We have both been looking at walls.

I think you are beautiful. If God would have given me eyes to see sooner!

He is very lucky, whoever he is.

I would like to know the real you.

Okay, so I have basically always gotten exactly the opposite of what it is I am asking for. Why? I don't know. All I know is that I am tired of it. Here I am acting like you are not beautiful and pissing you off for it. And there you are acting like you are perfectly happy and engaged and getting married, and could care less about anyone else PERIOD! It's like, someone amazing is standing right here but if I get with her then everyone will just be like they are TOO perfect. And unless things are hard to deal with then why do them? It's like I might as well never tell this beautiful girl she's beautiful because everyone already knows it. When really, all's I'm doing is fighting what everyone is thinking is going to happen. Jay and Shannon. And that's only for the mere fact of looks. They have no idea who we really are and so would assume that we love each other because of our looks, and what kind of example would that be making right? Looks aren't everything. We know this. We're just surrounded by ugly people I guess. HAHAHA.

While things stew let's move on to one of our more colorful employees, Miss Marge.

Marge has worked for Waffle House for over seven years. She is opening her own chapel, courtesy of her husband. Now, back in the day, Miss Marge's husband was a truck driver. He had taken out a loan for his semi from some unknown agency and had been paying on it as he worked. As times moved forward business got slow and he was nearly forced to sell his tractor trailer. Miss Marge, being the faithful brute that she is, continued working at the Waffle House to pay the bills and increasingly began to portray her problems on others. One thing I *can* say for Marge is, when she enters the establishment in the mornings, the place seems to take on a lighter air. She may, in fact, actually carry a little bit of the light of the creator with her after all.

Anyhow, eventually, an older man and a distinguished lady would enter one morning and offer Marge an open ear. Her story would start from the beginning and end thirty minutes later with no mention of her financial troubles at the time. Marge is just being good ole faithful Marge. The couple enjoys her service and her conversation and leaves her a fifty dollar tip! Thirty minutes later the couple returns to the Waffle House after driving around town and calls miss Marge outside to discuss something with her. Five minutes later she returns with a five thousand dollar check in hand as a 'Love Gift' that the couple claimed GOD told them to give to her ... she had saved her husbands truck! AND NO ... The check didn't bounce. Unbelievable? Believe it!

# A Rotten Choice

By: Chan and Shannon

Why is it once you start off on an undesirable track it is so hard to turn back right? Even after having been raised right and schooled, still children will turn to the dark side just to follow suite. Shannon's little boy toy that she met would cause her all kinds of grief over the next couple of years. The bad boy is always a females choice at first, so we can't blame her, but eventually, he'll wear her down and she'll turn her sights to money. This bad boy, caused a local some unforgettable trouble that would chase him to his grave.

We'll call him Chan, as opposed to the chink-a-link sound a handful of change makes as you shake it in your right hand. Chan, Shannon's boyfriend, was out having a great time with his buddies. Driving around in his new Catholic girlfriend's car, playing the tunes and finding some weed. He's the talk of the town in his own mind.

Shannon is working at the local Waffle House, earning tips. The customers give her hell, no doubt due to her good looks and young body. She flaunts what she's got. She's just got dismissed from a Catholic school where she never belonged to begin with. Now she's got a man, is having lots of premarital sex, and is making money just for looking good.

"Screw that prim and proper church stuff. I can do what I want, when I want. Barron won't fire me. Tell him I broke the mop, it won't matter." She says with a matter-of-fact expression. She quickly walks to the other end of her section as to stay busy while no body notices. She's on a high from the selfish things she's done and she rides it like a surfer on a tsunami.

Chan is rounding the corner into the Wal-Mart with his buddies on board as he spots a homeless man walking near the edge of the street. The man is toting his few belongings and walks with a sullen stride, his head drooping toward the ground in humble humility.

The music is blaring in the little Honda and the guys inside are pointing at the bum laughing as Chan swerves into the mud puddle nearby splashing the homeless man's pants and shoes. Chan slows the car down grinning at his friends.

"What are you doing now, man?" One of Chan's passengers wail, with still constant laughter.

"Hang on." Chan says as he throws the car in reverse and backs slowly until coming close next to the man who is now wiping the mud from his trousers. Chan leans out the window enough for the man to hear that his snude comment is directed right at him, "Hey man, will you suck my dick for a dollar?!" Chan slams the car in drive and peels forward laughing.

The Waffle House, his destination, is only seconds ahead in the same parking lot. He slides around the 90 degree turn and finds a parking space. The guys all pile out of the car and rowdily find their way into the establishment, joking about the man and shoving one another. Approaching their usual booth, Chan motions for them to sit down and waves his girlfriend over for some service. Maybe they can get the hook up on some free food while they're here,

*Chan is so cool.*

Shannon turns from the table she is serving, ignores the cooks call for her to come ad get her order that is ready, and approaches Chan. He pulls her into the booth next to him, "Hey baby! You working hard? Your man could use some grub." Shannon leans against him, oblivious to everyone's gawking stares and thoughts of her selfishness. The food for her last table sits by the grill getting cold, and the cook feels the eyes of the guests on him like he should deliver the food.

The cook is busy cooking four more orders and tries to shake it off, "Shannon, order up!" He repeats.

Chan and Shannon are joking around and his friends begin recounting their humiliating the bum in the parking lot as the door chime rings. A customer has entered the building for his cup of coffee. His pants soiled with mud and his knapsack over his shoulder.

A knapsack hits the seat of a chair right inside the entrance of the Waffle House and Chan begins laughing and pointing as the soiled man blurts out, "Hey boy! You know the dollar you were talking about, well if you're man enough to degrade your elders, why don't we step outside and seal the deal?!" Shannon recoils as if the man has threatened her and looks toward large Trixie for some support. Chan is still busy smirking but now sits in silence. The homeless man smells slightly of booze and continues, "You think your life is perfect and you can just go around saying whatever you want? Let's go little boy, and I will show you a thing or two!"

Trixie is walking over to come between the man and Shannon who's still sitting in the booth, now pressed firmly to her boyfriend. Her last customers food still sits, now ice cold by the grill operator, "I think you need to leave. You've been drinking."

Shannon slides out of the booth gripping her cell phone and sneaks slowly behind Trixie, dialing the police. The man looks beyond Trixie and says, "I came in here for my cup of coffee and I am not gonna sit here while the boy gets his jollies over me!" Trixie begins escorting the man out of the building and Chans face grows into a smile, as he whispers something to his friends.

The man is now outside of the Waffle House arguing with Trixie over her unfair treatment of him as the local police officer pulls up. The officer can smell the booze on the man and he is obviously homeless. Trixie does her number on the policeman, not letting the bum get a word in edgewise. The homeless man, now unable to argue his point, gets put into the cruiser.

Shannon comes outside and backs up Trixie with her best innocent recounting of the story, "The man came in and started shouting at me, and frightened me for no reason." Two young employees against one homeless drunk, the rest is history. The down-on-his-luck hobo gets to spend the next months in a cell.

The cruiser pulls away as the waitresses reenter the Waffle House. The line cook yells again, "Shannon, your food!" Shannon runs around the counter and finally delivers the families food to the table. The family eats the ice-cold food in silence and leaves no tip. Shannon's tsunami just got bigger and she is having the ride of her life. The next few weeks will be full of ego for the teenage couple and if life returns full circle they had better enjoy it, because they will eventually pay in full for their *rotten choice*.

## THE VICTIM

It was around midnight when the homeless man walked in the front door. Until that night I didn't realize how much Shannon deserved the unhappy marriage she was in route to.

Shanique and I had already finished our duties and were sitting at the low bar. We greeted the man as we did every one, with a warm welcome. The man was dressed in corduroy and slippers. His hair was a mess of brown locks and he spoke with only a solitary tooth in the middle of his upper gum line. Right in the center, that tooth hung, it was by far his most memorable attribute. Beyond that, I must say he was at least clean shaven and probably in his late forties.

He pulled up a chair close to us and requested a cup of coffee. Shanique obliged by waving me in the direction of the pot. Tonight was a very slow night, you know, the kind of night that makes you feel like you'd rather be on the front lines of a war than at the low bar in lonely Waffle House? As I poured the man his coffee he put his change on the counter to pay. I asked him how his night was.

"Someone stole my tent." He says. "I just got out of jail a while back and had finally got my tent set up, and someone stole it." He mumbled through his tooth.

I was feeling inquisitive and Shanique was gonna play along so I plopped down beside the dusty traveler and lended my ear.

"It's too cold out there to be without a tent and I hoped you two would let me stay in here for a bit." He says.

I am game due to my project and Shanique couldn't care less as long as she doesn't have to get up for the next four hours. I tell him, "Of course, the heat is free. We have been dead for an hour, tell me what's troubling you." The man sees my book on the table that has just been published and asks me about it.

When you tell someone you are a writer you get one of two responses. Either they will ignore the comment all together, or they will admire you a bit and look to see what they can gain from their meeting you. This time it was the later that played out.

"You know." He says, "I really ain't suppose to be in here." His body sways a bit but he pulls himself together and looks my way, "I got banned from this place about a year ago by some little girl calling the cops on me."

My ears perk up, I immediately think that the girl he may be talking about could be Shannon. I have much respect for laws and rules, but more for honesty, so I let the man continue.

"About a year ago, I was flying a sign out in front of Wal-Mart trying to pick up some Alms and when the sun got too much to bear I was headed here to have a cup of coffee. Now, I admit I had been drinking a bit, I am homeless and there is a reason for that, I am an alcoholic. But what that boy done was in no way right to do to any man, regardless."

He pauses long enough for me to ask, "What boy?" He sips his coffee, stirs, and sips again. "I don't know if you have ever been down on yourself but I was at this point and to top it off, this Chinese boy in a little car drives by with his friends hanging out the window gawking at me. They pull up next to me and stop. The boy asks me, 'Will you suck my dick for a dollar?' Then they pull around the corner and park at this Waffle House where I am headed."

The man sighs and drops his head toward his coffee cup. I feel a tinge of anger well up inside me toward teenagers and their cruelty. "Are you serious?!" I ask.

"Yeah. He's trying to be funny I guess for his friends. But I was going into Waffle House to get a coffee and now I would have to sit there in disgrace just to get out of the sun. So I had HAD it! I walked in and said, 'Hey BOY! You wanna do that deal you were talking about? Step out to the parking lot and let's get busy!' I was trying to teach the kid some manners, ya know?"

I am tuned into the guys story and nod. He continues, "The boy was sitting with his friends and that little waitress Shannon, who I only guessed was his girlfriend. The waitress goes to the back and calls the law to the Waffle House. When it is all said and done with, I am escorted to jail for three months for causing a disturbance."

My mouth was still open from astonishment. Shanique finally breaks her silence with, "I knew that girl was notin' but a lil' bitch."

The story made me think back a few nights when I had been working with Trixie and Shannon:

It was late and we had a new trainee on the floor. Chris was a teenager but he was a hard worker. He was starting off serving because he had got on with Waffle House through his mom Randy who also worked here. I can remember the event vividly.

A table of four had come in and sat down. For the most part they were well behaved, considering it was Saturday night at a Waffle

House. The Grandma of the family seemed to be a bit inebriated, but all else was fairly normal. A few hoots and hollers came from the table once in awhile, but no vulgarity or racial slurs. They were just a family of four coming home from a good night out. Chris happened to be the one serving them, and being one of his first experiences with intoxicated individuals, he was more or less looking to Shannon and Trixie on how to handle the situation. I was busy at the grill when a young couple came in and sat in Trixie's section.

The next thing I know I hear Trixie's voice boom across the restraunt, "Are they bothering you? Please tell me they're bothering you!" She was saying to the couple.

I could only guess she was talking about the only other people in the place, the table of four. I kept myself busy with my work thinking that Chris would be getting a pretty decent tip for dealing with the family's shenanigans if he kept up the good work. Meanwhile, a police officer is in route to our location.

That's right, a police officer. Trixie had told Shannon to call the police to come and calm down the intoxicated Grandma. Upon the shock of the officer's arrival, the family immediately apologized to everyone while explaining that they had no idea that there was a problem. I, with my back to the customers and busy at the grill was run amok with tension. I never heard anyone warn the family to quiet down, and I was totally in the family's cheering section. Eventually, the man of the group grew tired of hearing his mothers apologies for being obnoxious and blurted out, "Whoever called the cops sucks!"

At that point I couldn't help but laugh and raise my hand in agreement to his comment. Trixie, on the other hand, took the opportunity to fuel the fire and began arguing with the customer until finally telling them to just leave if they didn't like it. They took the bait and walked away agitated, half hungry, but by no means, less broke than when they arrived. There's no need in mentioning that Chris didn't get the tip he deserved. On top of that, we had a suspicious prank phone call for a to-go order later on, that cost us nearly sixty bucks in food, wonder who that could've been?

A few weeks after things had been simmering at the Waffle House I come in a bit before 9pm to start my usual ten hour night shift. Normally, I would like to sit and relax with a cup of coffee for a minute before jumping into my work, but this night is no different than any other. Marcus is sitting in a chair, laid back and relaxing when he sees me enter the door. As if he has been busy all night long, he jumps up and runs to the back. I know already what's running through his mind, namely, 'Jay's here, time to jet'.

I make an attempt to procure a cup of joe when he returns from the back with his jacket, "Yo man, the doors been tagged so I caint take out that trash ya know. I got things to do, I need to be working on this record deal."

I grab the coffeepot and begin to pour. It is twenty till nine. I look nonchalantly his way, "Aight, but I'm fixin to sit and enjoy a cup of coffee for I clock in." I say.

"Okay then man, everything's done, I'm out." He disappears out the front door in an instant.

I look at Anne who is sitting at the low bar before her shift, "Well, I guess that means I need to clock in!" I say sarcastically.

I have a lot of respect for Anne. She is the kind of person that everyone hates, just because she's perfect. I wouldn't be surprised to find out that she's been conducting her own Waffle House research project all along, as well. If she isn't, she is a true gem with skin as thick as rhinoceros hide. Hell, I wouldn't be surprised if I end up married to her! I have jogged with Anne on a few occasions but on many more occasions have heard innumerous accounts of her bad reputation. Everything from whore to stalker, but my experience of her has always been perfectly pleasant. I think an alternate title to this book could be 'the Gossip House', if anything.

Anne rolls here eyes and returns a sarcastic, "Right." To my previous statement about clocking in.

Marcus is always leaving early. He leaves the store in horrific shape and obviously doesn't care what others think of him while he's not around. He has an incredible knack for music but he won't slow down long enough to ever be successful. All I can say about Marcus is:

God bless him. If it weren't for him I wouldn't have shit to do all night long!

*"border scambled plate... smothered chunked and capped.... Hwwwaffleee on two."* Comes Bell's voice from somewhere down the line. Cup in hand, I turn toward the grill and start moving to the back to grab a dirty apron, but only after giving another sarcastic roll of my eyes to Anne sitting there staring. I see her stir as I walk away.

Bell's voice reminds me of sandpaper against grit. Making out her words is like trying to make out the picture on an old tube TV set on channel 99. You eventually just *assume* that the elbow or shoulder that you are seeing coming through to you, as many different colors and incoherent static, is a glimpse of a beautiful woman's tit and just handle your business.

Also on the floor is Chris's mom, Randy. The clock is ticking and everyone is ready to get out of this house and head to their home, if you know what I mean. Randy, for the most part, is a fairly nominal lady. She's done a good job raising her kids, or letting them raise themselves, and she works hard all day.

I am tying my apron in the back and focusing on deciphering Bell's call when Randy busts out with her usual statement, "Whelp, that's about it. Everything's done around here, sink's still broken but there's nothing I can do about that. I'm 'bout ready to clock out and get home. Y'all know I caint miss my wrastlin'! Uhn Uh." She pulls the ties to the back of her apron and slides another dish rack into place, "I just gotta see my John Cena. I caint be having myself stuck up in here for too long."

Randy is finishing her side work and doing her drawer count. She'll be headed for the door once everything is in its proper place as well.

It isn't thirty minutes until the shift has been changed and now only 3rd occupies the 'ole Waffle House. Pretty Ms. Perfect Anne, me, and Chris, Randy's son.

On this particular night an oddity occurs. In walks none other than the newly hired Tim. I say newly hired, but this guy probably knows more about the Waffle House drama that has went on here in the past five years than any one of us three. The only reason Tim got a job here at the Awful is because he sat at the other location day in and day out for nine months everyday his girlfriend worked. His girlfriend manages the other Waffle House in town, but to any onlooker over the past nine months you'd bet it was him. From clock in to clock out, he was there. Eventually, being shorthanded would land him a job as a greeter (how ironic), and he will eventually make his way through the ranks to cook.

I shoot a friendly glance to Tim as he sits at the high top. I have something on my mind and so does he. Here I stand thinking to myself that I may, in fact, have been at one point or another, one of the people he was worrying so much about hitting on his girlfriend. This thought rolls around in my mind as I realize that my research project is coming to a close.

I am still on a mission to do the right thing, and in my mind, that means alleviating some of the stress on this poor man's shoulders. I listen to a bit of his troubles for a while as he sips his coffee slow, and then I make the decision to come clean.

I walk to the back where my backpack is neatly hung on a well bent spoon, remove from it a copy of 'As the Waffle Burns' and return to the high bar. I fold the page the page that you're reading this instant inward and tell him to read the conclusion *misunderstood.*

Passing him the open book, I pat Chris on the shoulder and tell him to never stop chasing his dreams. As I walk by Anne her eyes meet mine and for a split second she wonders if she ever really knew me at all. The door that reads, "Have A Nice Day. We'll See You Tomorrow." Shuts silently behind me in its ever present state of hopefulness, over shadowed by it's uncounted memories of disappointment.

# MISUNDERSTOOD

By: Jay

~Tim glances back at the book and begins to read~

That's when I met her, the Australian. I knew it from the moment I laid eyes on her, she was the one, my final ticket. My boarding pass, my unburnt bridge in to the pearly gates of blissful heaven and a life of perfection. Her name was Amy, 20 years old and just as sweet as guava jelly. I had a plan from the start. I knew I was going all the way this time, I had been hurt too many times in the past, and had done my share of hurting as well. I figured my Karma had expunged itself finally and I wasn't making the same mistake twice!

I *did* tell her I loved her a bit soon, but at least we didn't have sex on the first date. That would wait for date two. She had just moved to America from down under less than two years ago, and had since been givin the USA run around. Guys screwing her and dumping her, using her, etc. She was always totally honest with me, even down to the point that when I said I loved her she told me that we were moving too fast and to say I liked her a whole lot instead. This I did for weeks, but she knew what my eyes really said.

It was on a Wednesday afternoon, after work had finally let us off. She had been having a horrific day.

I walked her to her car and, as we stood in the doorway, I removed from my pocket a certificate, "I was saving this for your birthday but I think maybe now is the time."

She took it from my hand. I had bought a star in the astrologic registry and named it after us so that when she looked up she would always remember us. She hugged me and then looked at me differently than I had ever seen. It was this night that she finally told me that she loved me.

Remembering how she had made me retract my first admonition of love, I reminded her, "You don't love me, you're just excited. *We* don't say 'I Love You' unless we truly mean it."

She didn't let go. "No. I mean, I love you, I truly love you. I know you, and I love you." a shake of her head seemed to make it real for her. Then she kissed me.

"She loves me!" I say to my co-workers as I re-enter the building laughing. She loves me."

Days turned to months, and months into years. Her next birthday was approaching and I knew exactly what I wanted to get her. I had been searching high and low and finally found the perfect gift on-line.

Who would have ever thought you could purchase a genuine acre of land on the moon? Well I found a web-site where you could. In case of global evacuation and extra terrestrial colonization you can reserve your one-acre spot of land on the moon. More for the mere fact that I wanted to be able to say that I had bought her the moon and the stars, than the practical application—I got it certified.

It wasn't a month after her birthday that I began to notice spots showing up around her labia. More and more began appearing over the next week until I finally had to mention something to her in bed.

"Baby." I said, "You got something going on down there that don't look right."

She sits up and says, "I know, I have been noticing it too. It has been burning a little bit lately and I don't know why."

I am in this relationship until the end, no matter what, I had already decided that on day one. So I tell her that we will stop having sex for a couple of days and see if it gets better, or what. A couple of days pass and she is not complaining about the burning anymore, but after a few times in the sac she starts up again.

"Let me take a look." I say. I have always been good on a computer so the first thing I do is look it up on Google when she's not around. I find a couple of similarities that look like HPV, which is an STD.

The next time I am alone with her in private we talk. I can see worry in her eyes, and I definitely am not safe from whatever it is that she has because I have been coupling with her for years, so I tell her that I love her and that if something turns up on me then we will go to the clinic. Two weeks later, I notice a bump.

The clinic sucks. Some nurse tugging on your unit and poking at you. She tells me the bump is an anomaly of some sort and not to be worried. So I tell her that the girl in the next room is my girlfriend and she walks out. When she returns she informs me that what Amy has is definitely HPV and that if I had been having sex with her, *which I have,* then I should have it to. She advises me to stop having unprotected sex with this girl immediately.

Amy is in tears as we leave. I tell her that everything will be fine, and that I am here for her, and that we will get through this together. Over the next few weeks, countless hours are spent at the clinic with her, while she is getting a freezing treatment and they are monitoring me. Her life sucks, but I would be by her side through it all and never place a moments blame.

I had bought this girl the moon and the stars and I was eventually planning on asking her for a Son. It would never happen.

A whisper around work is that she has been sitting late nights with a chubby customer who dressed like a thug and had just gotten released from prison a few months back. Our time together is getting strange and she is becoming distant.

One day, the night after I had set Amy and her mom up with a candle light dinner, I was relaxing on the couch when her phone rang. She walks into the other room to answer. My mind flips a switch and I know she's hiding something. Later, I sneak a peek at her phone and see his name on caller ID 'Chad'. Who knows how long she had been stepping out on me.

We worked at the same on opposite shifts lots of the time, I only figured that the tears she cried the first day at the clinic, were tears of sorrow, for me, after she leaves me for the man she contracted the disease from.

I will never know if I have HPV. It is undetectable in men. Thus far I have had no outbreaks five years later, and now they offer a shot to women which prevents contraction of the HP Virus. But at the time that this occurred, none of that was available and I simply felt a hand lay down upon my head from GOD and heard his voice loud and clear say, "Jay, you will never give or get love again with a clean conscience." And since, I haven't.

*Misunderstood* is a story explaining my reasoning for not having sex until marriage. Yet others have tales of their own. In the end I will be called the Male Whore of Waffle House, who is desperately chasing every sorry working women there. But, in fact, I am a man that expresses Love the only way I know is perfectly safe. That is, not to make it at all. I suppose when everyone sees me as a player and not as a Whole Heart, then I reckon anyone contained within these texts could, just as well, and may be,

*MISUNDERSTOOD.*

# A SOUTHERN FRIED SEARCH FOR GOOGLE ADWORDS

About a week after the end of my 'Waffle House Research Project' came to an end, I returned to pick up my paycheck and say my farewells to a crew and customers who served up my inspiration, diced and topped.

Barron was working late, which was a change from his normal morning shift. The sun was setting and a small lull in business granted us an opportunity to have a seat together.

"I saw that you got your book done. I read it. It was good. It was funny too, but not exactly what I had expected."

"Well, I write it how it comes, Barron."

"I know you loved working here. I have some bad news for you though." he says.

"Oh, here goes." I said.

"Upper management says that you will be on the no rehire list. They have a crazy idea that you were trying to sabotage the business."

"Are you kidding me? This is the second time I have worked for the company, I like it so much. I can't help that it is colorful."

"Well, apparently the owner's nephew is releasing a book about his life in the Waffle House industry."

"Whoa, wait a minute. I have been up front about this whole book, the entire time I have been writing it. I even had hopes of mass marketing it on the tables of the Waffle Houses."

"Yeah, well that's the thing." he says, as he pulls out a sealed package of table toppers for the family member's new book.

"You're not kidding me." I say bleakly ... Then after some thought, "I suppose they went to advertise on Google and saw that I had already utilized all of the Google adwords and adspace for Waffle House keywords, huh? That probably rubbed them the wrong way."

"I don't know, maybe. These are suppose to go out on the tables next week during the release."

"Well it's been a real pleasure, Sir. I only assume upper management was relayed the message about my writing a book at the beginning of my employment?"

He looks at me with a telling sideways smirk.

"It was fun."

As I pull the door to my truck closed, I take one last mental picture through the window for a fond farewell. Pulling through the Wal-Mart parking lot, out toward the highway, I see the flickering lights of the big yellow sign. A few letters missing, in its usual manner as the 'W' goes permanently dark – reminding me again, of *her*.

# Waffle House Regulars

# Which One Are You?

*1. You have to order your hash browns smothered and covered, but eatem' too late and they'll come out scattered and splattered.*

"Will I have my hash browns scattered, smothered, or chunked?"

-Either way I'll take my brain Fried.-

-Gloves… nuff said. This is *not* your ordinary house! Nor should it be—

-If you don't get the warm and fuzzy feeling during your visit, associated with the memory of your aunt smoking a cigarette while she makes your waffles in your double wide, then they're probably not doing it right.

Ahh, that's better☺

Jim Gaffigan said it best, "Picture a road-side gas station's restroom—that serves waffles. Okay, you've been to a Waffle House."

"I have had a waffle here every morning for the last 60 years."

-Sad.-

"I am at a Waffle House, so I actually fit in."

-Still,     You can't help but cross your eyes when you talk to her!-

"She don't look notin like me! So she ain't ma daughter! But we're together."

-Friends or child abduction?-

Working at the Waffle does sometimes have its perks, well besides being able to drink and smoke on duty.

Donnie Wahlberg left a $2,000 tip for this crew!

*2. I've seen a gun four times in my life—*

*three of those times were in a Waffle House, and the majority were held in the hands of men who were naked!*

The only place you can get into a bar fight and not be at a bar, and then become famous for it!

Really, this was no bar fight. James Shaw disarmed an active shooter at a Waffle House.

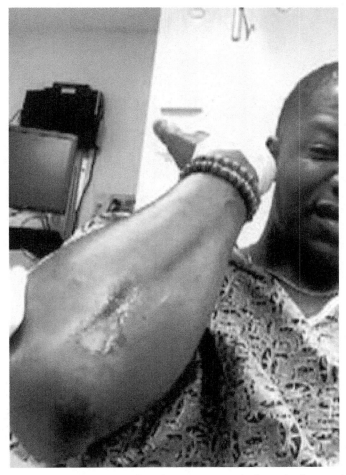

His gofund me hit $50,000 after the event, much from hollywood stars.

*This is suppose to be a funny section, but many people lost their lives that day and this man was a true hero! So was everyone working and visiting there that evening.*

As much as Waffle House gets criticized, an event like this really shows why we love the place. Everyone is family and we all share a common home here. *Nobody comes in our house alone.*

"I have done found a home until they figure I'm lying my ass off and charge me for a refill."

"If all else fails I will just say I am suppose to meet someone here."

-What'd it take for me to talk ya out of an order of biscuits and gravy?-

*3. In Atlanta, all directions start with, "Go down Peachtree..." and include the phrase, "When you see the Waffle House..."*

"Hey there. I know exactly what you're talking about. I have done plenty of that in my lifetime."

-No matter that I'm dirty and smell like a bum's nut sack, but let me join in on your conversation so I may pick up a ride from ya later.-

"Oh yeah. Just close your eyes for a second and imagine everything as pure energy."

-That's it, now open your eyes, and you can see fairies.-

*4. Waffle House is the perfect place to go when you're missing mama and grandma and want somebody to call you 'baby' and 'sugah' while they serve you food that you KNOW isn't good for you but tastes soooo right!*

"Don't you dare play a Waffle House song!  One more number one hundred and I am gonna snap!"

-I told you!-

-This speaks leaps and bounds about our music-

"Would you like that double capped?"

"I'll have an order of hash browns with no 'shrooms please!"

-And I thought I was excited about *eating*!-

"Meat lovers' pork chops please!"

"Is the pork chop dinner come with three pork chops?"

-We're waiting on…………...

You guessed it. Pork chops!-

Stages of Waffle House

-Early Years

Stages of Waffle House
- Later Years

"Dude! You burned the lady's waffles! Those gals don't want those waffles dark!"

-Might I suggest NAIR for men?-

"Cheap ass manager running third on a skeleton crew."

-Our Trajectory-

"You're guaranteed to receive at least half of your order"

"Yes you still have to pay, and no 'your looks' aren't legal tender"

-If all of them could look this good-

-But they can't-

"Yes, that's a wedding cake coming out of the back room."

-...and yes, those are wedding rings in the waffle.-

"And yes, that is her in her wedding dress."

-Could you be any more loving?-

"The excitement at Waffle House goes on and on."

-And on and on…-

"She may be the largest thing going at Waffle House…."

-But she's got nothin' on the lady in the cowboy boots and blue dress
standing behind her!-

"I would like to point out the strict policy we have on mustache only"

-No teasing, her hair really was that big!-

*5. You might be a redneck if; on the 4th of July you spend it at the waffle house beside a drunk while waiting to get your pastor out of jail (true story).*

"No, this is not Halloween."

-Just another normal night at the Waffle-

"Check out the double waffle!"

-Food quality?  Enough said!-

"We *are* the local bar."

-Dry county-

*6. If you plan to buy 105 Waffle House restaurants, also plan to grow a mullet and start selling meth.*

"I never leave the house."

-Can I get a discount?  I use to work here-

"And finally, our crowning achievement:
Kid Rock visits the Awful Waffle!"

-And then gets into a fight while he's there!-

-Yep. That's Waffle House for ya.-

# Waffleosophy

# Why did we come here?

*1. In order to make an omelet, ya gotta crack a few eggs.*

*Are we all a couple of eggs sunny-side-up, or just an order scrambled?*

Life is full of little disappointments. Though, some may disagree, aren't they really just temporarily basking in the happy-go-lucky feeling of whatever their present moment might contain? We all eventually die and experience disappointments. Some individuals are just really good at condoning forgetfulness through the art of focused mental distraction through occupation. As much as we may wish that it is possible for life to be lived in total harmony, from start to finish, it will never be so.

There are two quite different assumptions we can make about the universe and its possession of both good and bad experiences. The first is that the universe or God, is a single entity and both experiences are part of it. The second, is that the universe or God, is in fact, two separate entities--one entity which is goodness, and another that is evil.

In the latter assumption of a bilateral God, we would endeavor, our entire lives, to move far enough away from the evils during our experience in hopes of eradicating the thought and even memory of that side of the universe entirely. By the end, through focus, being left only with the good universe to boot.

In the former belief, (the belief that all is one) only a single possibility could assume that the one universe or God were actually good in nature. The ingrained requirement being: by the end of one's existence the evil be entirely overcome and its usefulness expired.

# 2. Don't cry over spilt milk!

Happiness is something that can only be maintained through mental and emotional sacrifice. Theologians will debate that sacrifice and happiness are two entirely differing sides of emotional spectrum— especially when those theologians are getting something for their opinions! Their idea of happiness and sacrifice may in-fact be as simple-mindedly synonymous to the phrase 'give and get'. or 'loss and gain'.

Religious and spiritual sects are separated into two basic beliefs on loss and gain. Of course, there are those who maintain belief in an entity, possibly self-regulated meta-physically and, who maintains a weighted perception of the individual as they make choices throughout daily activities. Then there are also those who believe that everything has been stewed up from some primordial soup and that no one judges actions of individuals because everything is just stuff, and we are mere electrically charged meat.

*Pleases take note:*
I make loose comments and statements of each belief, not to ridicule one or the other, but rather to be most Just as possible in my writing.

A gentleman has saved his bonuses for two years to take a trip and see the world's largest waffle next June. Approaching the event, his wife informs him that their daughter needs two thousand dollars to get into her summer program in high school, which might help her on her journey to achieving her dream of a famous dancer one day. Both men decide to sacrifice their solo-dream-trip in lieu of their daughter's hopes and dreams. But the question posed is: *What will each get out of it?*

The Christian looks into his wallet, at the ticket counter, pulls out his money, sniffs the warm air—while imaging the scent of a large syrupy waffle—and after a moment of detached pleasure, followed by a brief feeling of bereavement, places the money back in the billfold while surrendering his trip as a sacrifice to god, and leaving then the line quite contented. Soon he is walking along the sidewalk and mentally giving thanks for his wife and daughter, the money he has earned, the opportunity for his daughter's adventure, and patting himself on the back for a sacrifice toward the greater good. Furthermore, he then flips a coin into the beggars cup—not a usual action of his—as he passes to remind himself that every sacrifice, no matter how minute, brings him closer to heaven.

The Atheist looks at his wallet while standing in line at the ticket counter and imaginatively compares his daughter's trip to his own. Finding her trip—and his wife's mood thereafter the decision—more rewarding, he then places the money back in the billfold and exits the line. At best his mood is left moot—hoping that later his sacrifice will pay off under some cause-and-effect disguised as a misnomer—and at worst he departs emotionally disturbed with anger or jealousy. He later absently passes by the rattling can-holder on the corner—not his usual action—in no mood to incur further losses.

Each of these individuals posses the same organs—A stomach, a brain, lungs, a heart, and a spine—while they think and make their sacrifices. Those organs, which they both identically possess are at constant work toward a common goal as well. They strive to function to their best ability.

Yet, if the Thoughts or Minds of each differing individual—possessing in himself his own beliefs—are to be viewed as a *thing* (such as an organ), and not as most view them—as mere *Instances*—then does the Christian man's organ not function more efficiently than the one of the Athiest man's which offers no reward through release of positively charged endorphins and discourages gaiety, which resulted in the Christian additional action of supporting his fellow man?

# 3. Fine words produce no waffles.

*Love your waitress because happiness is in forgiving and forgetting*
*—She'll forget. So, be prepared to forgive☺—*

May it be that forgetfulness is the secret of the stars? If it is, and you find that secret to life and existence in a waffle house book, you are most definitely not the kind of person who will remember that said secret, then furthermore, apply it, and even if you happen to break free of that stereotype, then would you not be simply, in-turn, violating the greatest secret of the stars themselves anyhow?

Since we have discovered that the religious man benefits more from his sacrifices by maintaining a positively active and healthy state of mind, let us assume that our God, which we endeavor to be alike to,—indeed are even said to be made in the image of—also would benefit from a positive outlook on any negative situation he found himself in as well.

Could our once and forever solitary—existing only in the void—God, momentarily aware of his exquisite loneliness in a state of unity, have discovered that by simply busying his mind with stories he could forget about his nonphysical existence and essentially place that forgotten fact on a shelf to one day be discovered again through death? If so, would it not be the ultimate goal of such a lonely god to eternally be free of this fact of nonexistence through the trick of the mental disillusion? Furthermore, would a god, who'd forgotten his solitude and immortal nonexistence which had mistakenly found himself jailed or maimed in his illusion—which had become so real—, only find escape through remembering his initial conclusion of nonexistence, and retroactively feel reluctance in shelving all of his stories in exchange for a clean slate?

Another question to pose is: Would a god who'd discovered his power to manifest this forgetfulness through losing the mind in his internal dialogues begin having trouble doing so when the secret had been revealed? And finally, would that fear, manifest through trouble, not threaten forever being stuck in one state of physicality or the other of non; possibly keeping the god from ever merging the two aspects of his own creator-self and his creation?

Forgetting is the greatest trick in the universe. Memories are changed every time we recall them. A memory that has been reminisced over 60 times in sixty years will be more corrupt than a memory that is 60 years old and recalled only a single time on the 60th year. Our happiest moments are the times that we are furthest from our sourest memories, and butter pecan ice cream tastes sweetest when we've forgotten its flavor entirely.

Thoughts. The only things faster than light. Contemplation. The only form of energy whose transformation is not understood. Distraction. The only things that keeps our thoughts from contemplating our eventual and inevitable demise. Together they free us from the fear of death—could those three *gifts* not potentially have saved our creator from suffering his eternal loneliness?

Potential.

The only word in the human language that contains infinite possibility within its own utterance; the only energy that could ever have started the whole  experience.

We all know energy can neither be created or destroyed, it can only change form. But the potential is in you.

# Closing

Like all things, the passages you have read herein will sweeten as you time goes on and the memory fades. In that afterthought, we leave you in syrupy sorrow. Let us now take a moment to remember those who have come before us- the waitresses, the cooks, the management, the owners, the customers, the law enforcement, the medical staff, the first responders, the heroes… and the victims and their families. Warm a seat at Waffle House and continue to enlighten yourself to humanity. I've always said that Enlightenment is the temporary possession of infinite knowledge. All things are meant to eventually be forgotten, and in that knowledge—and in its own definition—those things we forget we in-turn place out there somewhere *for the getting once again.*

God Bless you all, and God Bless the Waffle House.

# THE END

## "Y'ALL COME BACK NOW!"
## "SEE YA TOMORROW!"

I hope you have enjoyed your journey with us. Thank you for reading 'As the Waffle Burns'. We hope that we have inspired some laughter and we are always open to comments and suggestions. So, please, tell us how we can improve. Visit our website: www.asthewaffleburns.com for opportunities in reading and in publishing. Feel free to also connect with us on facebook.

END

Get more books by the author of As the Waffle Burns at:

Amazon

Thank you for enjoying As the Waffle Burns

This book has been published by Bookflurry.com

Find more titles by the author at

Amazon.com

For More Information on As the Waffle Burns publications, and events please

Visit Us


asthewaffleburns.com

Made in the USA
Columbia, SC
19 August 2018